Free Verse Editions
Edited by Jon Thompson

MIRRORFORMS

Peter Kline

Parlor Press
Anderson, South Carolina
www.parlorpress.com

Parlor Press LLC, Anderson, South Carolina, 29621

© 2020 by Parlor Press
All rights reserved.
Printed in the United States of America
S A N: 2 5 4 - 8 8 7 9

Library of Congress Cataloging-in-Publication Data on File

978-1-64317-130-2 (paperback)
978-1-64317-131-9 (pdf)
978-1-64317-132-6 (ePub)

1 2 3 4 5

Cover design by Lisa Beth Anderson and Logan Evasco.
Cover photo Untitled from the series *Skin* by Kate Hoffmann.

Parlor Press, LLC is an independent publisher of scholarly and trade titles in print and multimedia formats. This book is available in paperback and ebook formats from Parlor Press on the World Wide Web at http://www.parlorpress.com or through online and brick-and-mortar bookstores. For submission information or to find out about Parlor Press publications, write to Parlor Press, 3015 Brackenberry Drive, Anderson, South Carolina, 29621, or email editor@parlorpress.com.

Contents

Psalms

I	*5*
II	*6*
III	*7*
IV	*8*
V	*9*
VI	*10*
VII	*11*
VIII	*12*
IX	*13*
X	*14*
XI	*15*
XII	*16*
XIII	*17*
XIV	*18*
XV	*19*
XVI	*20*
XVII	*21*
XVIII	*22*
XIX	*23*
XX	*24*

End-Stops

Whatever	*27*
Malediction	*28*
Double Cliché	*29*
Proverbs	*30*

Contents

    Life & Death   *31*
    SIGECAPS   *32*
    Pajamalaise   *33*
    Rubber Stamp   *34*
    Funhouse Mirror   *35*

Monologues

    The Living Dead   *39*
    Procrastinator   *40*
    Shapeshifter   *41*
    Narcissist   *42*
    Trumpeteer   *43*
    Daredevil   *44*
    Capitalist   *45*
    Theorist   *46*
    Convalescent   *47*
    Catcaller   *48*
    Opportunist   *49*
    Sadist   *50*
    Visionary   *51*
    Apostate   *52*
    Worrier   *53*
    Impetuist   *54*
    Futurist   *55*
    Skeptic   *56*
    Flirt   *57*

Studies

    Conservation   *61*
    Hypnology   *62*
    Microeconomics   *63*
    Narratology   *64*
    Accounting   *65*
    Risk Management   *66*
    Cognitive Science   *67*
    Mathematics   *68*

Contents

    Disaster Research   *69*
    Genealogy   *70*
    Anatomy   *71*
    Radiophysics   *72*

Votives

    Blue Yonder   *75*
    Field Guide   *76*
    A Bouquet for Amy Clampitt   *77*
    In Memory Of   *78*
    Lament   *79*
    Planetary   *80*

Notes   *82*
Acknowledgments   *83*
About the Author   *87*
Free Verse Editions   *89*

Mirrorforms

Psalms

I

Since I'm not mine to keep,
who is my true owner?
Am I just one more goner
playing house from sleep to sleep?

I have two stoops to sweep,
one east, one west exposure.
I'm tidying toward foreclosure
since I'm not mine to keep.

II

Lord, let this worry break.
I'm trying to outwait time,
debunk sleep's paradigm
and wake wake   wake   wake   wake

into my absence, shake
the wavering of my mind
before I'm undefined—
Lord, let this worry break.

III

How can I be true
when you keep vanishing?
I get one verse to sing—
who do I sing it to?

I've learned to look for you
in the blur of ringing strings.
You could be anything.
How can I be true?

IV

I'm learning how to ask
to serve the way you listen.
This silence is a lesson—
my manner has been brusque.

Forgive me. At the risk
of losing your affection
I question my instructions.
I'm learning how to ask.

V

Is there a place for me
deep in a secret pocket
of your black leather jacket
to pass eternity?

I'm flexible as money,
trim as a sugar packet,
thin as a one-way ticket—
Is there a place for me?

VI

Maker of patterns and shapes;
Calligraphist of the spine
of the serpent: You define
the vine as a line and the grape

as a prison the wine must escape.
Engineer: by your design
we break down at three score and nine:
Maker of patterns and shapes.

VII

What if I just let go—
Is it so far to fall
from nothing to nothing, all
the way from yes to no?

To hang or be hung, though
the scaffold is Sky-High,
is a strung-out way to die.
What if I just let go?

VIII

Does it have to be just me?
Can't someone else come too?
I belong to no one. You
who made what it is to be

estrange yourself from me
by being undying. Who
can I give this living to
if it has to be just me?

IX

I've turned the wrong way twice—
Come set my shoulders straight.
Command my thighs to wait
for the spurs of your advice.

Take back my voice. Disgrace
what atom of me might
wonder at left and right.
I've turned the wrong way twice.

X

Lord, put your mark on me
so no one claims me first.
Even Cain, accursed,
had hard proof you could see

his soul's reality.
Alone on all the earth
he knew what he was worth.
Lord, put your mark on me.

XI

If not me, Lord, then who?
Can I be sure to know him
if he looks strange, or show him
the face that I show you?

How should the new me be?
Shall I be his and yours
to put down on all fours?
And who, Lord, if not me?

XII

Can I do you some good?
Are you too flush for favors?
Do all your favorite flavors
sweeten your spoon when they should?

Once, I was hungry. Blood
foamed in a wooden saucer,
warm as your hand. Master,
can I do you some good?

XIII

Too much is not enough—
Please let there be more more.
I've been a hungerer
however I've been stuffed.

Your giving-hand is rough.
I bend to it. Two sore
lips are my true reward.
Too much is not enough.

XIV

Think of me as your stray
bullet, cease-fire twitch
whose ricochet won't scratch
a name from a list, or pay

a blood-debt. Runaway
heir to the Whole Shebang,
alias "The Pranceling"—
think of me as your stray.

XV

If I'm to hunt for you
ahead of my own flesh,
twist my wrist with the leash
while hot meat saunters through

till your horn commands Pursue,
if ever it does, I'd best
get good at being chased.
—If I'm to hunt for you.

XVI

I've never been your man.
Since I could choose
to love you or refuse,
I've been a courtesan

to an immense Amen,
spreading my good news
in six-inch platform shoes.
I've never been your man.

XVII

For you I'd strip down bare,
but won't you give me cover?
Dallying with forever
is a high-risk affair.

I've tried new underwear
to tempt a tempted lover,
made my whole wardrobe over.
For you, I'd strip down bare.

XVIII

I feel you entering,
slickering in   then through—
forcing the issue. Who
are you to wear my ring

without asking? You'll bring
trouble if I refuse.
—But before I can choose
I feel you entering.

XIX

I'll show you you through me.
I wonder—will you be pleased?
Or sway like a man amazed
his I has been made III?

Facsimile of thee
but no true duplicate,
I was made to fade. Just wait—
I'll show you you through me.

XX

I make you in my image.
From the hem of your day-glo robe
to your hurt heart and trick rib,
you are pure human homage.

Could it be I do you damage
conceiving you? An act
of love can't be abstract—
I make you in my image.

End-Stops

Whatever

—whiffles your whirligig
—pips you —pops your Bud
—puts pepper in your pud
—prinks you —sprigs your wig

—waggles your thingamajig
—gets your giggle —packs your pipe
—makes your raisins ripe
—whiffles your whirligig

Malediction

Get the ditch-itch and die.
Go beddy-bye and stay there.
Take a header from your highchair.
Gobble the big sky-pie.

Pick out a permanent necktie.
Hire the gospel choir.
Make like a milk jug: Expire.
Get the ditch-itch and die.

Double Cliché

Scrubbed-up with the same soap.
Spit-shined by the same rag.
Buds from the same dime bag.
As twin as tan and taupe.

Double-duped by the rope-a-dope.
Hooked like an Eng-Chang eel.
Two shucked clams at the Raw Deal.
Scrubbed-up with the same soap.

Proverbs

The blue light burns out first.
The naked throat gets bit.
Because the key, the kite.
The mainsail breaks the mast.

To slow down time, go west.
Because the air, the lung.
With death and taxes, song.
The blue light burns out first.

Life

The is before the was.
The chemical machine.
The ssssss of the divine.
The "thinking-being" phase.

The Holocenic craze.
The oblivial divide.
The itch of the suicide.
The is before the was.

Death

That which doesn't change.
The glass eye in the sundae.
The guerdon of the workday.
The gangway to the Strange.

The Santa Barbara binge.
The way of Auntie Mack.
The secret in the tick.
That which does not change.

SIGECAPS

In the livery of winter.
Dissertating gray.
Satisfied to die.
Dangled by the panther.

Weeping underwater.
Feeling for the null.
Glassed off from the soul.
In the livery of winter.

Pajamalaise

The destination brunch.
The lovingkindness class.
The CRISPRed babyface.
The Sunday Funday paunch.

The housetrained Darwin's finch.
The burr mill loneliness.
The polyamorous kiss.
The desolation brunch.

Rubber Stamp

Take action / Take no action
Compel / Condone / Combat
"No comment." / "Could you repeat that?" /
(Accelerate redaction)

Fiction / ~~XXXXXXX~~
Ground-invade / Concede
Cut him / Let him bleed
Take action / Take no action

Funhouse Mirror

The drink the pill fell in.
The . in Kink.com.
The ink in the letter bomb.
The beard of Ho Chi Minh.

The bard of Ho Chi Minh.
The prank in the letter bomb.
The oink in Kink.com.
The pool the drink fell in.

Monologues

The Living Dead

Asleep with the light left on
I dream in animation:
I'm a zombie porno station.
Grubworms binge on the lawn.

Someone left the dog on
and it died. It's "on vacation."
We're all flying toward that nation,
asleep with the light left on.

Procrastinator

It's later than it was
when Christ slipped off to pray.
I was asleep that day.
Tonight I'm wired. NoDoz

is not my favorite buzz,
but the shaking makes me double.
There's a corpse at the kitchen table.
It's later than it was.

Shapeshifter

Whenever I want I change.
I can't be made to fix:
$x = x$ —Relax
while I do this brain exchange.

I binge at Buffet Strange:
What begins in little inklings
ends in new biggenings.
Whenever I want, I change.

Narcissist

A different difficulty
from each day's mirror-test
(Which way do I look best?)
might make my thoughts more pretty.

Self-study breeds self-pity.
Give me the will to choose
a less exacting muse,
a different difficulty.

Trumpeteer

You don't get more from me
so spare me the orphan porn,
the harelipped unicorn
stuffed in some poacher's display

beside a drowned refugee,
her head unscarved. I paid
to gas up the motorcade.
You don't get more from me.

Daredevil

I fall off the right way—
I put the bike to bed
then slide for my better side,
blowing a kiss to the DJ.

I get gauzed by applause. The day
I die my body bag
will be an American flag.
I fall off the right way.

Capitalist

Subdivide and conquer!
This side of Camelot
might yield a corner lot
to serve the Slurpee-drinker.

'Realators' and bankers
carve out their fixed percent
with Guinevere's consent:
subdivide and conquer.

Theorist

There is no private browsing.
-Unidentified-
ogles the F.B.I.
ogling your carousing.

Disgusting but arousing
.gifs you've long since trashed
still infiltrate your head-cache.
There is no private browsing.

Convalescent

Now that I'm pissing clear
I'm fit to love again.
Bailiff, put me in.
There are no victims here.

It's been a dirty year
since I got passed the mop.
The spigot's on non-stop
now that I'm pissing clear.

Catcaller

I do it to myself,
and not 'cause I can't help it.
I make my lips a pulpit
and testify the Wolf.

Of course I'd prefer *pelf*,
but that likes soft-sell tactics.
My gift is autocratics—
I do it to myself.

Opportunist

Elliott Smith

Give up the thing you love
but keep it in your sight.
Follow it home at night.
From a shadowy alcove

watch as one calfskin glove
slips off to withdraw a key—
then it goes inside with me.
Give up the thing you love.

Sadist

Maurice Manning

As dark as darkness gets—
I've turned a word that dark.
It was tricky. It took work.
With the tip of a cigarette

I tortured an alphabet,
blinding its eye. It sees,
now, an infinity:
as dark as darkness gets.

Visionary

I see what's almost there—
a book-shaped gap in a thought
or the sex in the statesman's obit,
cracks in the exosphere.

Let rubberneckers stare
at the fur the killer wore,
the flash of flesh at the tear.
I see what's almost there.

Apostate

Emily Dickinson

It might be easier
to make the door more strict,
double the doormen, act
at the contracted hour

as though no one were here,
grow quaintly derelict
with no Guest to evict.
It might be easier.

Worrier

I know what it must be
but I can't bear to check.
Playing patience with a short deck;
Counting back from infinity

until it's time to see
that no one hid. I've heard
even God has a safety word—
I know what it must be.

Impetuist

It takes so fucking long!
There's no time left to live.
Just as I slip a groove
I'm cueing some new song

and the beat goes dark. The bang
dangles on the buck.
One line drags three weeks' slack.
It takes so fucking long.

Futurist

Death was just something to do.
Nothing was something to feel.
Only the android was real.
God was all 0s and 2s.

Now we wake up with a bruise
in the shape of the morning before;
permafrost weeps like a sore.
Death is still something to do.

Skeptic

It happened anyway
as engineers played bridge
and Noah hit the fridge
and gave his dog away.

Me, I was on the freeway,
ice in my glass. I knew
what a trumped-up sun could do.
It happened anyway.

Flirt

Do you have time for me
out of your unweighed portion—
a grain, a gram's transgression
against eternity?

Next Saturday I'm free
for a transgression session.
After your due devotions
do you have time for me?

Studies

Conservation

Ernest Hemingway

Nothing is ever lost
but, missing a long time,
things earn a different name.
We learn it at our cost.

Hearts crossed and double-crossed
scar into asterisks:
*XO AT YOUR OWN RISK
Nothing is ever lost.

Hypnology

Edna St. Vincent Millay

Every bed is narrow
presently. Extra space
becomes a hiding place
lit up with blinking arrows.

Whoever your bedfellow,
there's only room for one
in Blackout Garrison.
Every bed is narrow.

Microeconomics

Bought hearts are hearts for rent.
Parceled safe away
until redemption day
earning their six percent,

some secretly repent
for their omitted sins
by taking strangers in.
Bought hearts are hearts for rent.

Narratology

Before the definitive wink;
After the errant hair
is fingersmoothed, and the mirror
queried and proved pink;

As the antepenultimate drink
rhymes with the prior four
and the pips in the dice cup blur...
Before the definitive wink.

Accounting

Wasted or well-spent—
the goodness goes both ways,
in seven-digit sprees
or seven decades' rent.

Renew the argument;
short-sell and make peace.
Our currency is loss,
wasted or well-spent.

Risk Management

Heinrich Heine

Never to have been born;
Torn out clean as a page
from the Domesday of your age;
Poofed like a hope; Reformed

preemptively; Affirmed
by infinite harmlessness;
Not dead-forever—less:
Never to have been born.

Cognitive Science

Death in the present tense
is gift-wrapped in abstraction,
a papered-over fiction
the peering mind invents.

Redressed to innocence;
raimented for election;
stripped naked by subtraction:
Death in the present tense.

Mathematics

The absolute of blue
is only made by minus.
Vein jay sea sky and iris
adulterate the hue

and must be purged. The true
blue that marries thought
with deed and word is not
the absolute of blue.

Disaster Research

Lazy eyes grow sharp
peeking between curtains
to save an arm's exertion
and keep a daybed dark.

Gauging the watermark
along the window brim
as a new storm pours in,
lazy eyes grow sharp.

Genealogy

James Merrill

Desires ungratified
break down into the flesh,
tangling in the mesh
of plaited nucleotides.

Some spike the lymph, or blood.
Others, more benign,
put kinks in the family line
who can't be gratified.

Anatomy

An artificial heart
through years of tinkering
can twitch like the real thing,
ticking out its quarts

aspiringly. What art
inked or improvised
could plausibly disguise
an artificial heart?

Radiophysics

Charles Wright

The station beyond silence
broadcasts in negative.
Each agitated wave
flatlines into balance.

Vowels and consonants
whose music moved through time
are posted in white frames
in the station beyond silence.

Votives

Blue Yonder

for Sydney

I can still feel your blue,
hard like the truth is hard.
It bruises me. No word
I know could soften you.

No word can bring you to.
On the flatlands of your death
your ripcord smile is myth.
I can still feel your blue.

Field Guide

In memory of Robert Perham

A true west-tending soul
is only seen at sunset,
and then in silhouette.
Yet, for this loss of detail

(black claw black throat black bill)
its flight is clear. Sky-
fatigue identifies
a true west-tending soul.

A Bouquet for Amy Clampitt

Wild Columbine.
Painted Trillium.
Bittersweet. Pink. Plum.
Coltsfoot. Dandelion.

Partridgeberry Vine.
Johnny-Jump-Up. Broom.
Laurel. Lindenbloom.
Wild Columbine.

In Memory Of

Mark Strand

Rain that passes in sleep.
The shadow of a quark.
A glint in the permanent dark.
More shallow than skin-deep.

The first uncounted sheep.
The crack between two hours.
That which the moment devours.
Rain that passes in sleep.

Lament

Will it be the sound of powder?
Of pollen? The smell of whiskey
in glasses three-years-empty?
The look of the air where you were?

If it can't be sent in a letter
or kept in a false-face drawer,
will it soften like a color?
Will it be the sound of powder?

Planetary

If only here were there—
If only if were were
if if were is, and where
you are and why and for

whose fire you fire were fire
underwater. Where prayer
takes on an atmosphere—
If only there were here.

Notes

"Opportunist" draws its repeating line from Elliott Smith's "Pitseleh"

"Sadist" draws its repeating line from Maurice Manning's Bucolics XLVII

"Apostate" draws its repeating line from Emily Dickinson's #405 ("It might be lonelier")

"Conservation" draws its repeating line from Ernest Hemingway's "The End of Something"

"Hypnology" draws its repeating line from Edna St. Vincent Millay's "Passer Mortuus Est"

"Risk Management" draws its repeating line from Heinrich Heine's "Morphine"

"Genealogy" draws its repeating line from James Merrill's "The Kimono"

"Radiophysics" draws its repeating line from Charles Wright's "Future Tense"

"In Memory Of" draws its repeating line from Mark Strand's "In Memory of Joseph Brodsky"

Acknowledgments

Thanks to the editors of the following journals in which these poems first appeared, sometimes in slightly different form or under alternate title:

32 Poems: "Funhouse Mirror," "SIGECAPS"

Able Muse: "Genealogy"

The American Journal of Poetry: "Convalescent," "Daredevil"

At the Inkwell: "Lament"

Belleville Park Pages: "Cognitive Science"

Blackbird: "The Living Dead," "Shapeshifter," "Visionary"

Cave Wall: "Life & Death"

Connotation Press: An Online Artifact: "Capitalist," "Flirt"

The Cortland Review: "Worrier"

Five Points: Psalm V, Psalm X

Hampden-Sydney Poetry Review: Psalm IV, Psalm VIII, Psalm XIV

Measure: "Disaster Research," "In Memory of"

Pleiades: Psalm I, Psalm III

Poetry Crush: Psalm XVII

Poetry Flash: Psalm XVIII, "Blue Yonder," "Double Cliché," "Pajamalaise," "Rubber Stamp"

Raintown Review: "A Bouquet for Amy Clampitt"

RHINO: "Procrastinator"

River Styx, 2015 International Poetry Contest First Prize: Psalm II, Psalm VI, Psalm VII, Psalm IX, Psalm XIII, Psalm XIX

The Rotary Dial: "Catcaller," "Opportunist," "Sadist"

Smartish Pace: "Accounting," "Anatomy," "Narcissist," "Radiophysics"

Southern Humanities Review: "Apostate," "Conservation," "Hypnology"

Southern Poetry Review: "Malediction," "Planetary"

Subtropics: "Futurist," "Theorist," "Trumpeteer"

Terrain.org: "Skeptic"

Think: Psalm XVI

Unsplendid: "Field Guide," "Mathematics," "Narratology"

I also want to thank Jon Thompson, David Blakesley, and everyone at Parlor Press/Free Verse Editions for believing in my book and for all the hard work of bringing it out into the world. I am deeply grateful to Lisa Beth Anderson and Logan Evasco for their book design and to Kate Hoffmann for allowing me the use of her photograph for the cover. Thanks to the James Merrill House, Amy Clampitt House, Kimmel Harding Nelson Center for the Arts, Marble House Project, Artsmith Orcas Island, and Joan and Greg Swanberg at the Mill House for critical time and support as I brought the manuscript to completion, with a special thank you to the angels of Stonington, Lynn and Jeff Callahan. I owe a debt of gratitude to Moira Egan and Bruce Snider for their willingness to so thoughtfully advocate for *Mirrorforms*, and to Mary Kinzie, Lisa Russ Spaar, and Eavan Boland for their unflagging encouragement and wisdom over many years. Thanks to my colleagues and friends in the Stanford Creative Writing Program, the University of San Francisco English Department, and Stanford University's Master of Liberal Arts Program for helping me to make space for my work, especially Christina Ablaza, Susan Steinberg, and Linda Paulson. I owe a special thanks to

George David Clark for his tireless support at *32 Poems* and to Andrew Hudgins who served as guest judge at *River Styx*. Thanks to Richmond Republic for always having a seat for me. Finally, this book would never have been possible without the incisive, honest criticism of fierce poets to steer it on its way—Kim Addonizio, James Arthur, Ben Gucciardi, Randall Mann, Doug Powell, Matthew Siegel, Greg Wrenn, and most of all, Brittany Perham—this one is for you.

About the Author

Peter Kline teaches writing at the University of San Francisco and in Stanford University's Master of Liberal Arts Program. A former Wallace Stegner Fellow at Stanford, he has also received residency fellowships from the Amy Clampitt House, James Merrill House, Marble House Project, Artsmith Orcas Island, and Kimmel Harding Nelson Foundation. His poetry has appeared in *Ploughshares, Poetry, Tin House*, and many other journals, as well as the *Best New Poets* series, the *Verse Daily* website, and the Random House anthology of metrical poetry, *Measure for Measure*. Since 2012 he has directed the San Francisco literary reading series Bazaar Writers Salon. He is the author of one previous poetry collection, *Deviants*, published by Stephen F. Austin State University Press in 2013.

Photograph of the author by Lisa Beth Anderson.
Used by permission.

Free Verse Editions

Edited by Jon Thompson

13 ways of happily by Emily Carr
& in Open, Marvel by Felicia Zamora
Alias by Eric Pankey
At Your Feet (A Teus Pés) by Ana Cristina César, edited by Katrina Dodson, translated by Brenda Hillman and Helen Hillman
Bari's Love Song by Kang Eun-Gyo, translated by Chung Eun-Gwi
Between the Twilight and the Sky by Jennie Neighbors
Blood Orbits by Ger Killeen
The Bodies by Christopher Sindt
The Book of Isaac by Aidan Semmens
The Calling by Bruce Bond
Canticle of the Night Path by Jennifer Atkinson
Child in the Road by Cindy Savett
Condominium of the Flesh by Valerio Magrelli, translated by Clarissa Botsford
Contrapuntal by Christopher Kondrich
Country Album by James Capozzi
The Curiosities by Brittany Perham
Current by Lisa Fishman
Day In, Day Out by Simon Smith
Dear Reader by Bruce Bond
Dismantling the Angel by Eric Pankey
Divination Machine by F. Daniel Rzicznek
Elsewhere, That Small by Monica Berlin
Empire by Tracy Zeman
Erros by Morgan Lucas Schuldt
Fifteen Seconds without Sorrow by Shim Bo-Seon, translated by Chung Eun-Gwi and Brother Anthony of Taizé
The Forever Notes by Ethel Rackin
The Flying House by Dawn-Michelle Baude
Go On by Ethel Rackin
Instances: Selected Poems by Jeongrye Choi, translated by Brenda Hillman, Wayne de Fremery, & Jeongrye Choi
The Magnetic Brackets by Jesús Losada, translated by Michael Smith & Luis Ingelmo
Man Praying by Donald Platt
A Map of Faring by Peter Riley

The Miraculous Courageous by Josh Booton
Mirrorforms by Peter Kline
No Shape Bends the River So Long by Monica Berlin & Beth Marzoni
Not into the Blossoms and Not into the Air by Elizabeth Jacobson
Overyellow, by Nicolas Pesquès, translated by Cole Swensen
Physis by Nicolas Pesquès, translated by Cole Swensen
Pilgrimage Suites by Derek Gromadzki
Pilgrimly by Siobhán Scarry
Poems from above the Hill & Selected Work by Ashur Etwebi, translated by Brenda Hillman & Diallah Haidar
The Prison Poems by Miguel Hernández, translated by Michael Smith
Puppet Wardrobe by Daniel Tiffany
Quarry by Carolyn Guinzio
remanence by Boyer Rickel
Rumor by Elizabeth Robinson
Settlers by F. Daniel Rzicznek
Signs Following by Ger Killeen
Small Sillion by Joshua McKinney
Split the Crow by Sarah Sousa
Spine by Carolyn Guinzio
Spool by Matthew Cooperman
Summoned by Guillevic, trans. by Monique Chefdor & Stella Harvey
Sunshine Wound by L. S. Klatt
System and Population by Christopher Sindt
These Beautiful Limits by Thomas Lisk
They Who Saw the Deep by Geraldine Monk
The Thinking Eye by Jennifer Atkinson
This History That Just Happened by Hannah Craig
An Unchanging Blue: Selected Poems 1962–1975 by Rolf Dieter Brinkmann, translated by Mark Terrill
Under the Quick by Molly Bendall
Verge by Morgan Lucas Schuldt
The Wash by Adam Clay
We'll See by Georges Godeau, translated by Kathleen McGookey
What Stillness Illuminated by Yermiyahu Ahron Taub
Winter Journey [Viaggio d'inverno] by Attilio Bertolucci, translated by Nicholas Benson
Wonder Rooms by Allison Funk